Predators

SPOTTED HYENAS

BY MEGAN GENDELL

WWW.APEXEDITIONS.COM

Copyright © 2024 by Apex Editions, Mendota Heights, MN 55120. All rights reserved. No part of this book may be reproduced or utilized in any form or by any means without written permission from the publisher.

Apex is distributed by North Star Editions:
sales@northstareditions.com | 888-417-0195

Produced for Apex by Red Line Editorial.

Photographs ©: Shutterstock Images, cover, 4–5, 10–11, 12–13, 14, 15, 16–17, 18, 19, 20–21, 22–23, 24, 25, 26, 29; iStockphoto, 1, 6–7, 8–9

Library of Congress Control Number: 2023910263

ISBN
978-1-63738-776-4 (hardcover)
978-1-63738-819-8 (paperback)
978-1-63738-900-3 (ebook pdf)
978-1-63738-862-4 (hosted ebook)

Printed in the United States of America
Mankato, MN
012024

NOTE TO PARENTS AND EDUCATORS

Apex books are designed to build literacy skills in striving readers. Exciting, high-interest content attracts and holds readers' attention. The text is carefully leveled to allow students to achieve success quickly. Additional features, such as bolded glossary words for difficult terms, help build comprehension.

CHAPTER 1
HYENAS ATTACK 4

CHAPTER 2
BONE CRUSHERS 10

CHAPTER 3
FIERCE HUNTERS 18

CHAPTER 4
HYENA LIFE 22

COMPREHENSION QUESTIONS • 28
GLOSSARY • 30
TO LEARN MORE • 31
ABOUT THE AUTHOR • 31
INDEX • 32

CHAPTER 1

HYENAS ATTACK

A group of spotted hyenas roam the **savanna**. They see a **herd** of zebras. The hyenas start chasing the herd.

It usually takes more than 10 hyenas to catch a zebra.

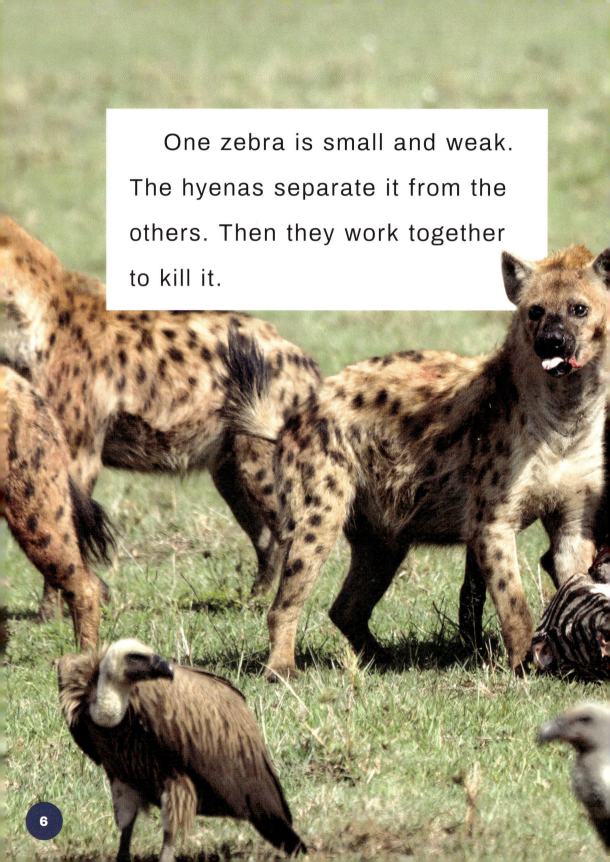

One zebra is small and weak. The hyenas separate it from the others. Then they work together to kill it.

Hyenas guard their prey so other animals won't steal it.

A LONG CHASE

Hyenas can run as fast as 40 miles per hour (64 km/h). They can chase their **prey** for a long time, too. All the running makes prey tired. Tired animals are easier for hyenas to catch.

More hyenas join the meal. The hyenas eat every part of the zebra. Soon, only tiny scraps of it are left.

FAST FACT

A hyena can eat up to 40 pounds (18 kg) of food in an hour.

Hyenas can chew through their prey's horns, hooves, and teeth.

CHAPTER 2

BONE CRUSHERS

Spotted hyenas are **mammals**. They live south of the Sahara Desert in Africa. They are found in savannas, forests, and even swamps.

Spotted hyenas look like dogs. But they are more closely related to cats.

A spotted hyena's fur is gray, tan, or yellowish with dark spots. Longer fur called a mane sticks up along its neck.

There are several different types of hyenas. The spotted hyena is the largest type. Spotted hyenas can weigh more than 155 pounds (70 kg). They grow about 2.7 feet (0.8 m) tall.

NOT REALLY LAUGHING

Spotted hyenas are sometimes called laughing hyenas. When they are scared or excited, they make noises. The noises sound like giggling. Spotted hyenas also growl, squeal, and grunt.

Hyenas are some of the only animals whose teeth can crack bones and eat the marrow inside.

Spotted hyenas have big heads with strong jaws. Their large teeth can break bones. Spotted hyenas also have long, strong legs.

FAST FACT
A hyena can bite through a bowling ball.

A spotted hyena's front legs are longer than its back legs. This helps the hyena carry large pieces of prey.

CHAPTER 3

FIERCE HUNTERS

Sometimes hyenas hunt alone. They kill small animals like birds and lizards. Hyenas can also eat bugs.

Hyenas hunt and kill most of the food they eat.

When hyenas hunt in groups, they attack bigger animals. Large prey includes buffalo, antelopes, and warthogs.

A group of hyenas can eat a whole 1,500-pound (680-kg) buffalo in just a few hours.

Groups of hyenas sometimes chase lions away from their food.

FACING DANGER

Hyenas have few **predators**. But sometimes lions kill hyenas. They might fight over the same food. Lions often take prey hyenas have killed. Lions also kill hyena cubs.

While hyenas mainly hunt, they can also be scavengers. They find and eat food that is already dead. They can eat **rotting** food without getting sick.

FAST FACT

Hyenas can eat hair and hooves. But they usually spit up these parts later.

Other scavengers such as vultures sometimes try to take hyenas' food.

CHAPTER 4

HYENA LIFE

Spotted hyenas live in groups called clans. The female hyenas are in charge. They are usually bigger than males.

One clan can include more than 100 hyenas.

Pairs of hyenas come together to **mate**. After a few months, females give birth. Later, mothers and cubs move to large dens. The dens are shared with other hyenas.

Newborn hyena cubs have dark fur with no spots. The fur color changes as cubs grow.

FAST FACT
Many females give birth to twin cubs.

Up to 20 cubs might live in shared dens.

25

Mothers care for their cubs for around three years. The cubs grow and get stronger. They also learn how to hunt.

KICKED OUT

After female hyenas have grown, they stay with their clan. Males leave to join another clan. As new members, these males have the lowest **status**. They eat last and might get only bones.

◀ At first, mother hyenas feed their cubs milk. Later, cubs begin eating meat.

COMPREHENSION QUESTIONS

Write your answers on a separate piece of paper.

1. Write a few sentences describing what hyenas eat.

2. If you were a hyena, would you rather hunt alone or with others? Why?

3. Which type of animal could a hyena hunt alone?

    A. buffalo
    B. lizard
    C. zebra

4. Why could tired animals be easier for hyenas to catch?

    A. Tired animals can't run as fast.
    B. Tired animals run farther.
    C. Tired animals fight back more.

5. What does **scraps** mean in this book?

The hyenas eat every part of the zebra. Soon, only tiny scraps of it are left.

    A. whole parts
    B. most parts
    C. small bits

6. What does **scavengers** mean in this book?

While hyenas mainly hunt, they can also be scavengers. They find and eat food that is already dead.

    A. animals that only eat plants
    B. animals that only eat prey they killed
    C. animals that eat prey they did not kill

Answer key on page 32.

GLOSSARY

herd

A large group of animals that live together.

mammals

Animals that have hair and produce milk for their young.

mate

To form a pair and come together to have babies.

predators

Animals that hunt and eat other animals.

prey

Animals that are hunted and eaten by other animals.

rotting

Falling apart after dying.

savanna

A flat, grassy area with few or no trees.

status

How important an animal is in a group.

BOOKS

Jaycox, Jaclyn. *Female Spotted Hyenas: Commanders of the Clan*. North Mankato, MN: Capstone Publishing, 2023.

Marie, Renata. *Hyenas*. Minneapolis: Kaleidoscope, 2023.

Sommer, Nathan. *Lion vs. Hyena Clan*. Minneapolis: Bellwether Media, 2020.

ONLINE RESOURCES

Visit **www.apexeditions.com** to find links and resources related to this title.

ABOUT THE AUTHOR

Megan Gendell is a writer and editor. She loves learning and writing about wild animals.

A
Africa, 10

C
clans, 22, 27
cubs, 19, 24–25, 27

D
dens, 24

H
hunting, 16, 18, 20, 27

L
laughing, 13
lions, 19

P
predators, 19
prey, 7, 18–19

S
Sahara Desert, 10
savannas, 4, 10
scavengers, 20

T
teeth, 14

Z
zebras, 4, 6, 8

ANSWER KEY:
1. Answers will vary; 2. Answers will vary; 3. B; 4. A; 5. C; 6. C